Charlie's Secret
Chocolate Book

Illustrated by Quentin Blake

PUF

PUFFIN BOOKS

Published by the Penguin Group
Penguin Books Ltd, 27 Wrights Lane, London W8 5TZ, England
Penguin Books USA Inc., 375 Hudson Street, New York, New York 10014, USA
Penguin Books Australia Ltd, Ringwood, Victoria, Australia
Penguin Books Canada Ltd, 10 Alcorn Avenue, Toronto, Ontario, Canada M4V 3B2
Penguin Books (NZ) Ltd, 182–190 Wairau Road, Auckland 10, New Zealand

Penguin Books Ltd, Registered Offices: Harmondsworth, Middlesex, England

First published 1997
1 3 5 7 9 10 8 6 4 2

Filmset in Adobe Janson

Reproduction by Anglia Graphics Ltd, Bedford

Made and printed in Great Britain by William Clowes Ltd, Beccles and London

British Library Cataloguing in Publication Data
A CIP catalogue record for this book is available from the British Library

ISBN 0–140–38676–9

All about Charlie and the Chocolate Factory

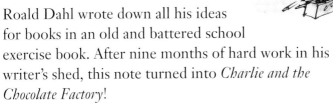

What about a chocolate factory that makes fantastic and marvellous things – with a crazy man running it?

Roald Dahl wrote down all his ideas for books in an old and battered school exercise book. After nine months of hard work in his writer's shed, this note turned into *Charlie and the Chocolate Factory*!

Charlie and the Chocolate Factory was Roald Dahl's second book for children. It was first published in the USA in 1964 and in Britain in 1967. With *James and the Giant Peach*, it marked the beginning of his climb to superstardom.

Charlie and the Chocolate Factory is now the best-loved children's book of all time, and sells all over the world – in countries as widespread as France, Holland, Thailand, Korea and Brazil!

Chocolate!

Everything you always wanted to know

The Swiss eat more chocolate per person than any other nation in the world.

Belgium is the third biggest producer of chocolate in the world.

Just like Willy Wonka, many Belgian chocolate makers keep their recipes secret.

Cocoa was discovered by the South American Indians over 3,000 years ago.

The word chocolate comes from *chocolatl*, the Aztec name for their chocolate drink.

The scientific name for cocoa means 'food of the gods'.

Cocoa beans were considered so valuable, the Aztecs used them as money – ten beans would buy a rabbit!

Originally, chocolate was used just as a drink. The Spaniards took cocoa to Europe from Mexico in the sixteenth century. They kept the recipe for drinking-chocolate secret for nearly 100 years!

In 1606 an Italian took the recipe to Italy, and chocolate drinking became popular throughout Europe.

There was a royal chocolate maker at the court of Louis XIV.

At first, chocolate was only for the rich. They drank it in 'Chocolate houses', which were like smart cafés.

The first chocolate factory in America was set up in 1765.

Cocoa powder is made from dried beans which are roasted and ground.

It takes a year's crop of cocoa beans from one tree to make just one tin of cocoa!

Cocoa pods are as big as rugby balls. They contain about thirty beans.

Factories can produce over five million bars of chocolate a day.

Charlie's Quiz

1   How many new kinds of chocolate bar has Mr Willy Wonka invented?

2   What did Prince Pondicherry ask Willy Wonka to do?

3   How do the chocolates and sweets come out of Mr Wonka's factory?

4   How many Golden Tickets are there altogether?

5   Who finds the second Golden Ticket?

6   What does Violet Beauregarde do all day?

7   What does Mike Teavee like doing best?

8   In what kind of chocolate bar does Charlie find his Golden Ticket?

9   What sort of coat does Willy Wonka wear?

10   Where are the most important rooms in Willy Wonka's factory?

11 How is the chocolate mixed?

12 What happens to Augustus Gloop?

13 What is Willy Wonka's private yacht made from?

14 Which is the most important room in the whole factory?

15 Why does Violet Beauregarde turn into a gigantic blueberry?

16 Who pushes Veruca Salt down the rubbish chute?

17 Why is the lift so special?

18 What happens when Willy Wonka presses the UP AND OUT button in the lift?

19 What does Mike Teavee look like when he leaves the factory?

20 What present does Willy Wonka decide to give Charlie?

Turn to page 29 for the answers – if you really have to!

Could YOU be an author?

Roald Dahl said:

'The job of a children's writer is to try to write a book that is so exciting and fast and wonderful that the child falls in love with it.'

Have you got what it takes to be an author? You might well have – it's just that you don't know it yet!

Believe it or not, Roald Dahl only found out he could write by accident. At the age of twenty-six he was 'discovered' by C. S. Forester, author of the Captain Horatio Hornblower stories. From that moment, he never stopped writing.

But it's not easy. These are the qualities Roald Dahl suggested you will need if you are going to become a writer:

1 You should have a lively imagination.

2 You should be able to write well. By that I mean you should be able to make a scene come alive in the reader's mind.

3 You must have stamina. In other words, you must be able to stick to what you are doing and never give up.

4 You must be a perfectionist. That means you must never be satisfied with what you have written until you have rewritten it again and again, making it as good as you possibly can.

5 You must have strong self-discipline.

6 It helps a lot if you have a keen sense of humour.

7 You must have a degree of humility. The writer who thinks that his work is marvellous is heading for trouble.

Point 4 is crucial. Roald Dahl spent nine months writing *Charlie and the Chocolate Factory*. There was a first draft, then a second, then a third, and so on. With each rewrite the story would get better and better. Some bits were added in, other bits taken out – it is just as important to know what to leave out of a book as it is to decide what to put in!

Roald Dahl cut out a whole chapter from the final version of *Charlie and the Chocolate Factory*. It was called 'Spotty Powder'. He also took out two children, and changed the ending completely!

Read 'Spotty Powder', and the other bits you'll never find in *Charlie and the Chocolate Factory*. Can you see why Roald Dahl was right to leave them out?

'Spotty Powder' and other bits you'll never find in Charlie and the Chocolate Factory

Spotty Powder

This chapter was originally included in Charlie and the Chocolate Factory. *But there were too many naughty children in the earlier versions of the book, so 'Spotty Powder' – and the revolting Miranda Piker! – had to be dropped.*

'THIS stuff,' said Mr Wonka, 'is going to cause chaos in schools all over the world when I get it in the shops.'

The room they now entered had rows and rows of pipes coming straight up out of the floor. The pipes were bent over at the top and they looked like large walking sticks. Out of every pipe there trickled a stream of white crystals. Hundreds of Oompa-Loompas were running to and fro, catching the crystals in little golden boxes and stacking the boxes against the walls.

'Spotty Powder!' exclaimed Mr Wonka, beaming at the company. 'There it is! That's it! Fantastic stuff!'

'It looks like sugar,' said Miranda Piker.

'It's *meant* to look like sugar,' Mr Wonka said. 'And it *tastes* like sugar. But it *isn't* sugar. Oh, dear me, no.'

'Then what is it?' asked Miranda Piker, speaking rather rudely.

'That door over there,' said Mr Wonka, turning away from Miranda and pointing to a small red door at the far end of the room, 'leads directly down to the machine that makes the powder. Twice a day, I go down there

myself to feed it. But I'm the only one. Nobody ever comes with me.'

They all stared at the little door on which it said MOST SECRET – KEEP OUT.

The hum and throb of powerful machinery could be heard coming up from the depths below, and the floor itself was vibrating all the time. The children could feel it through the soles of their shoes.

Miranda Piker now pushed forward and stood in front of Mr Wonka. She was a nasty-looking girl with a smug face and a smirk on her mouth, and whenever she spoke it was always with a voice that seemed to be saying, 'Everybody is a fool except me.'

'OK,' Miranda Piker said, smirking at Mr Wonka. 'So what's the big news? What's this stuff meant to do when you eat it?'

'Ah-ha,' said Mr Wonka, his eyes sparkling with glee. 'You'd never guess that, not in a million years. Now listen. All you have to do is sprinkle it over your cereal at breakfast-time, pretending it's sugar. Then you eat it. And *then*, exactly five seconds after that, you come out in bright red spots all over your face and neck.'

'What sort of a silly ass wants spots on his face at breakfast-time?' said Miranda Piker.

'Let me finish,' said Mr Wonka. 'So then your mother looks at you across the table and says, "My poor child. You must have chickenpox. You can't possibly go to school today." So you stay at home. But by lunch-time, the spots have all disappeared.'

'Terrific!' shouted Charlie. 'That's just what I want for the day we have exams!'

'That is the ideal time to use it,' said Mr Wonka. 'But you mustn't do it too often or it'll give the game away. Keep it for the really nasty days.'

'Father!' cried Miranda Piker. 'Did you hear what this stuff does? It's shocking! It mustn't be allowed!'

Mr Piker, Miranda's father, stepped forward and faced Mr Wonka. He had a smooth white face like a boiled onion.

'Now see here, Wonka,' he said. 'I happen to be the headmaster of a large school, and I won't allow you to sell this rubbish to the children! It's . . . it's criminal! Why, you'll ruin the school system of the entire country!'

'I hope so,' said Mr Wonka.

'It's *got* to be stopped!' shouted Mr Piker, waving his cane.

'Who's going to stop it?' asked Mr Wonka. 'In *my* factory, I make things to please children. I don't care about grown-ups.'

'I am top of my form,' Miranda Piker said, smirking at Mr Wonka. 'And I've never missed a day's school in my life.'

'Then it's time you did,' Mr Wonka said.

'How dare you!' said Mr Piker.

'All holidays and vacations should be stopped!' cried Miranda. 'Children are meant to work, not play.'

'Quite right, my girl,' cried Mr Piker, patting Miranda on the top of the head. 'All work and no play has made you what you are today.'

'Isn't she wonderful?' said Mrs Piker, beaming at her daughter.

'Come on then, Father!' cried Miranda. 'Let's go down into the cellar and smash the machine that makes this dreadful stuff!'

'Forward!' shouted Mr Piker, brandishing his cane and making a dash for the little red door on which it said MOST SECRET – KEEP OUT.

'Stop!' said Mr Wonka. 'Don't go in there! It's terribly secret!'

'Let's see you stop us, you old goat!' shouted Miranda.

'We'll smash it to smithereens!' yelled Mr Piker. And a few seconds later the two of them had disappeared through the door.

There was a moment's silence.

Then, far off in the distance, from somewhere deep underground, there came a fearful scream.

'That's my husband!' cried Mrs Piker, going blue in the face.

There was another scream.

'And that's Miranda!' yelled Mrs Piker, beginning to hop around in circles. 'What's happening to them? What have you got down there, you dreadful beast?'

'Oh, nothing much,' Mr Wonka answered. 'Just a lot of cogs and wheels and chains and things like that, all going round and round and round.'

'You villain!' she screamed. 'I know your tricks! You're grinding them into powder! In two minutes my darling Miranda will come pouring out of one of those dreadful pipes, and so will my husband!'

'Of course,' said Mr Wonka. 'That's part of the recipe.'

'It's *what*!'

'We've got to use one or two schoolmasters occasionally or it wouldn't work.'

'Did you *hear* him?' shrieked Mrs Piker, turning to the others. 'He admits it! He's nothing but a cold-blooded murderer!'

Mr Wonka smiled and patted Mrs Piker gently on the arm. 'Dear lady,' he said, 'I was only joking.'

'Then why did they scream?' snapped Mrs Piker. 'I distinctly heard them scream!'

'Those weren't screams,' Mr Wonka said. 'They were laughs.'

'My husband never laughs,' said Mrs Piker.

Mr Wonka flicked his fingers, and up came an Oompa-Loompa.

'Kindly escort Mrs Piker to the boiler room,' Mr Wonka said. 'Don't fret, dear lady,' he went on, shaking Mrs Piker warmly by the hand. 'They'll all come out in the wash. There's nothing to worry about. Off you go. Thank you for coming. Farewell! Goodbye! A pleasure to meet you!'

'Listen, Charlie!' said Grandpa Joe. 'The Oompa-Loompas are starting to sing again!'

'Oh, Miranda Mary Piker!' sang the five Oompa-Loompas dancing about and laughing and beating madly on their tiny drums.

'Oh, Miranda Mary Piker,
How could anybody like her,
Such a priggish and revolting little kid.
So we said, "Why don't we fix her
In the Spotty-Powder mixer
Then we're bound to like her better than we did."
Soon this child who is so vicious
Will have gotten quite delicious,
And her classmates will have surely understood
That instead of saying, "Miranda!
Oh, the beast! We cannot stand her!"
They'll be saying, "Oh, how useful and how good!"'

The Missing Children

Originally, seven children
were going to visit
Mr Wonka's
Chocolate Factory.
Five of them you know:

Charlie Bucket
A NICE BOY

Herpes Trout
A TELEVISION-CRAZY BOY (he became
Mike Teavee in the final version!)

Violet Beauregarde
A GIRL WHO CHEWS GUM ALL DAY LONG

Veruca Salt
A GIRL WHO IS ALLOWED TO HAVE ANYTHING THAT SHE WANTS

Augustus Gloop
A GREEDY BOY

MISSING

These two didn't make it:

Marvin Prune
A CONCEITED BOY
Miranda Mary Piker
A GIRL WHO IS
ALLOWED TO DO
ANYTHING THAT SHE
WANTS

The Whipple-Scrumpets

Have a look at an early version of the Oompa-Loompas' song about greedy Augustus Gloop, and compare it to the one which actually appears in Charlie and the Chocolate Factory. *Can you spot the differences? Bet you never knew the Oompa-Loompas were originally called the 'Whipple-Scrumpets'!*

The Whipple-Scrumpets . . . began dancing about and clapping their hands and singing:

> '*Augustus Gloop! Augustus Gloop!*
> *The great big greedy nincompoop!*
> *How long could we allow this beast*
> *To gorge and guzzle, feed and feast*
> *On everything he wanted to?*
> *Great Scott! It simply wouldn't do!*
> *And so, you see, the time was ripe*
> *To send him shooting up the pipe;*
> *He had to go. It had to be.*
> *And very soon he's going to see*
> *Inside the room to which he's gone*
> *Some funny things are going on.*

But don't, dear children, be alarmed.
Augustus Gloop will not be harmed,
Although, of course, we must admit
He will be altered quite a bit.
For instance, all those lumps of fat
Will disappear just like that!
He'll shrink and shrink and shrink and shrink,
His skin will be no longer pink,
He'll be so smooth and square and small
He will not know himself at all.
Farewell, Augustus Gloop, farewell!
For soon you'll be a caramel!'

'They're teasing,' Mr Wonka said, shaking a finger at the singing Whipple-Scrumpets. 'You mustn't believe a word they say.'

Charlie's Chocolate Shop

At one time, Charlie and the Chocolate Factory *was going to end very differently! This was the ending in an earlier version:*

The shop has been finished now, and it is the most beautiful chocolate shop in the world. It occupies a whole block in the centre of the city, and it is nine storeys high.

Inside it, there are moving staircases and elevators to take the customers up and down, and no less than one hundred ladies, all dressed in spotless gold and chocolate uniforms, are there to serve behind the counters. They will sell you anything you want from a single little blue bird's egg with a tiny sugary bird inside it to a life-size chocolate elephant with huge curvy tusks and a chocolate elephant driver sitting on its back.

And Charlie Bucket, coming home from school in the evenings, nearly always brings along with him about twenty or thirty of his friends and tells them that they can choose anything they want – for free.

'It's my shop,' he says. 'Just help yourselves.'

And they do.

Isn't it amazing how much a book can change before it is published?

Do you still fancy being an author? Then grab a pencil (or sit down at the computer!), start writing, and just don't stop!

Strawberry-flavoured Chocolate-coated Fudge

YOU WILL NEED:

8 x 10 inch (20 x 25 cm) shallow baking tin
greaseproof paper
large saucepan
sugar thermometer
cutters

1 lb (450 g) caster sugar (cane)

4 oz (100 g) unsalted butter

6 fl oz (175 ml) evaporated milk

a few generous drops of pink food-colouring

a generous ¹/₂ tsp (2.5 ml) of strawberry food-flavouring (Supercook)

4 oz (100 g) melted chocolate for dipping

Makes enough for ten greedy children

1 Line the tin with buttered greaseproof paper.

2 Put all the ingredients except flavouring and colouring into a large heavy-bottomed saucepan and place over a low heat.

3 Stir occasionally. Once the sugar has dissolved, gently boil the mixture and now stir all the time (to prevent sticking and burning on the bottom of the pan). Place the sugar thermometer into the saucepan and boil the mixture to a soft ball 245°F (118°C). This takes about five minutes.

4 Take the pan off the heat, stir until the bubbles subside and then add the flavouring and the colouring.

5 Beat rapidly with a wooden spoon until the mixture thickens and becomes granular, approx. three minutes.

6 Pour the fudge into the lined tin and leave to set. If necessary, smooth with a palette knife dipped into boiling water.

7 With shaped cutters, cut out the fudge and dip one side into the melted chocolate, or decorate with piped chocolate creating different patterns as in illustration.

Butterscotch

YOU WILL NEED:

large saucepan
large jug
whisk
cling film

1 oz (25 g) butter

1 oz (25 g) caster sugar

1 oz (25 g) golden syrup

1 pt (600 ml) fat-free milk

3 fl oz (75 ml) natural yoghurt

Makes approx. 1¼ pt (3–4 mugs)

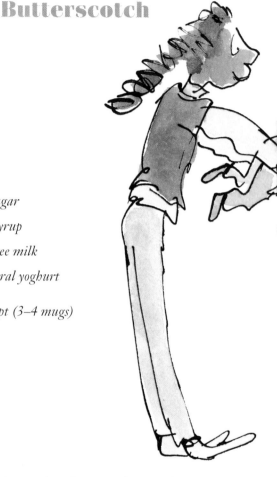

1 In a saucepan, over a low heat, melt together the
   butter, sugar and golden syrup, stirring all the time
   until the sugar has dissolved (about 10 minutes). Add
   a little milk to the pan, then transfer to a jug.

2 Whisk in a little more milk, approx 2 fl oz (50 ml) followed by all the yoghurt.

3 Whisk in the remaining milk.

4 Cover with cling film. Chill before serving.

Roald Dahl

Roald Dahl was born in 1916 in Wales of Norwegian parents. He was educated in England before starting work for the Shell Oil Company in Africa. He began writing after a 'monumental bash on the head' sustained as an RAF fighter pilot during the Second World War. Roald Dahl was one of the most successful and well known of all children's writers. His books, which are read by children the world over, include *James and the Giant Peach*, *Charlie and the Chocolate Factory*, *The Magic Finger*, *Charlie and the Great Glass Elevator*, *Fantastic Mr Fox*, *The Twits*, *The BFG* and *The Witches*, winner of the 1983 Whitbread Award. Roald Dahl died in November 1990 at the age of seventy-four.

Quentin Blake

Quentin Blake, OBE, was born in London in 1932. After graduating from Downing College, Cambridge, he went on to do a post-graduate Certificate in Education at the University of London. He was a cartoonist for *Punch* magazine from 1949 and an illustrator for the *Spectator* and subsequently many other magazines. He did his first illustrations for children in 1960, and has illustrated many of Roald Dahl's novels. He has also written and illustrated a number of his own books. For several years he was Head of Illustration at the Royal College of Art. He lives in London.

Answers to Charlie's Quiz

1   More than two hundred

2   Build him a chocolate palace

3   Through a special trap door in the wall

4   Five

5   Veruca Salt

6   She chews gum

7   Watching television

8   A Whipple-Scrumptious Fudgemallow Delight

9   A tailcoat made of plum-coloured velvet

10   Underground

11   By waterfall

12   He falls into the chocolate river and gets sucked up a pipe into the strawberry-flavoured chocolate-coated fudge room

13   An enormous hollowed-out boiled sweet

14   The inventing room

15   Because she chews a piece of the three-course-dinner chewing-gum

16   The squirrels

17   It can go in any direction, and visit any room in the factory

18   It flies out through the roof of the factory

19   About ten feet tall and thin as a wire

20   The whole chocolate factory

PICTURE BOOKS

Dirty Beasts (*with Quentin Blake*)

The Enormous Crocodile (*with Quentin Blake*)

The Giraffe and the Pelly and Me (*with Quentin Blake*)

The Minpins (*with Patrick Benson*)

Roald Dahl's Revolting Rhymes (*with Quentin Blake*)

FOR OLDER READERS

The Great Automatic Grammatizator

Rhyme Stew

The Vicar of Nibbleswicke

The Wonderful Story of Henry Sugar and Six More

PLAYS

The BFG: Plays for Children
(*adapted by David Wood*)

Charlie and the Chocolate Factory: A Play
(*adapted by Richard George*)

Fantastic Mr Fox: A Play
(*adapted by Sally Reid*)

James and the Giant Peach: A Play
(*adapted by Richard George*)

QUIZ BOOKS

The Roald Dahl Quiz Book 1
(*Richard Maher/Sylvia Bond*)

The Roald Dahl Quiz Book 2
(*Sylvia Bond/Richard Maher*)

The
Roald Dahl Registered Charity
Foundation No. 1004230

Throughout his life Roald Dahl gave of his time and money to help people in need. When he died, his widow, Felicity Dahl, established The Roald Dahl Foundation to continue this generous tradition. The Foundation's aim is to serve people in the UK in three major areas:

- **Literacy**, because it was Roald's crusade. Literacy is the most basic educational tool. It is also the passport to hours of pleasure. For many reasons, some people and some groups need extra assistance to help them achieve this essential skill. The Foundation offers grants to a diverse group in this area.

- **Neurology**, because brain damage has severely affected the Dahl family. Neurology funds specialize in the areas of epilepsy and head injury. In addition to our ongoing programme of individual grants to people in financial hardship, the Foundation grants funds to specially identified projects.

- **Haematology**, because leukaemia was the cause of Roald's death. Our haematology grants target areas where funds are particularly hard to come by, but where the need is undeniably great. In addition to many individual grants, the Foundation supports large scale projects.

All monies donated to the Foundation are directed where they are required – to people in the UK with specific needs. If you would like to know more about us, or help the Foundation in its work by making a donation, then please write to us direct:

The Roald Dahl Foundation
92 High Street
Great Missenden
Buckinghamshire HP16 0AN
England